GRAMMAR
PRACTICE BOOK

Grade 2

**Macmillan
McGraw-Hill**

New York • Farmington

CONTENTS

LEVEL 6, UNIT 1

Charlie Anderson

Henry and Mudge

Luka's Quilt

Carry Go Bring Come

The Mysterious Tadpole

The Goat in the Rug

Henry's Wrong Turn

Swimmy

The Sun Is Always Shining Somewhere

Willie's Not the Hugging Kind

Nine-in-One, Grr! Grr!

The Wednesday Surprise

Dear Daddy . . .

Best Wishes, Ed

Puff . . . Flash . . . Bang!

Angel Child, Dragon Child

LEVEL 7, UNIT 2

Jamaica Tag-Along

The Best Friends Club

Our Soccer League

Princess Pooh

Come a Tide

The Sun, the Wind and the Rain

Llama and the Great Flood

A Curve in the River

IS IT A SENTENCE?

These are both sentences.

The cat jumps over Jack.

Is Jack sleeping?

Underline the one in each group that is a sentence.

1. a. The cat sleeps.
    b. The sleeps.
    c. The dog the cat.

2. a. Sam's cat.
    b. Sam for a cat.
    c. Sam is a cat.

3. a. Can the cat?
    b. Can the cat climb?
    c. Cat climb high?

4. a. Finds the dog.
    b. Min finds the dog.
    c. Min the dog.

5. a. Jack is sleeping.
    b. Jack over the cat.
    c. Jack to sleep.

6. a. Is sleeping late?
    b. Jill sleeping now?
    c. Is Jill sleeping?

7. a. Where is the cat?
    b. Where the cat?
    c. Where dog and cat?

8. a. My dog likes cats.
    b. Likes cats.
    c. My dog and cats.

8 | Level 6/Unit 1
Sentences

Extension: You may wish to have children describe a pet or other animal, using a complete sentence.

1

A SENTENCE IS A COMPLETE THOUGHT

Remember

- A sentence tells a complete thought.

woods

in the woods

a walk in the woods

The girls take a walk in the woods.

Circle each correct sentence.

1. It is raining.

2. The sun is not shining.

3. After the rain.

4. The clouds.

5. We will see a rainbow.

6. Jay builds a doghouse.

7. Emma has a hammer.

8. Maybe Emma and Jay.

9. The doghouse is finished.

10. A cat moves into the doghouse.

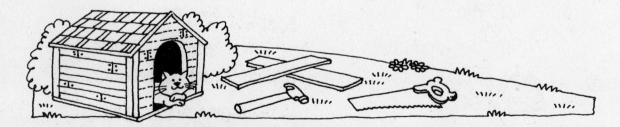

Extension: You may wish to have children suggest incomplete sentences that other children turn into complete sentences.

Level 6/Unit 1
Sentences

10

Macmillan/McGraw-Hill

STATEMENTS

Remember

- A statement is a sentence that tells something.
- It ends with a period.

I live with my father.   I live with my mother.

Which one is a statement? Underline the sentence that is a statement.

1.    **a.** Nadia hugs her mother.
   b. Nadia and her mother.

2.   **a.** Visits her father.
   b. Clare's father hugs her.

3.    **a.** Lots of tall buildings.
   b. Nadia lives in the city.

4.   **a.** Nadia forgot her brush.
   b. Her hair brush.

5.    **a.** Both Clare and Nadia.
   b. Both girls are laughing.

5

Level 6/Unit 1
Sentences: Statements

Extension: You may wish to have children tell something that happened this morning, using statements.

3

Macmillan/McGraw-Hill

QUESTIONS

Remember

- A question is a sentence that asks something.
- It ends with a question mark.

Have you found your lost frog?   Have you seen him?

Circle each sentence that is a question.

1. I have looked everywhere.   2. Your frog?

3. When did you lose him?   4. My frog has green stripes.

5. Is your frog brown?   6. Where have you looked?

7. Everywhere.   8. It's getting late.

9. Do you think he is all right?   10. Frogs like the outdoors.

STATEMENTS AND QUESTIONS

Remember

- A sentence gives a complete thought.
- A statement is a sentence that tells something.
- A question is a sentence that asks something.

Read the story. Then read the sentences. Choose the correct mark to put after each one. Fill in the circle next to the answer.

Hector and Luis are camping in the woods. They build a fire and cook dinner. Then they clean up. Finally, they go to sleep. Just before dawn, they hear a loud noise. They think it is a lion roaring. It is only a garbage truck.

1. Are Hector and Luis good friends _____

   (a.) ?
   (b.) .

2. Luis and Hector made their own dinner _____

   (a.) ?
   (b.) .

3. After they had dinner, they cleaned up _____

   (a.) ?
   (b.) .

4. Did the boys see a lion in the woods _____

   (a.) ?
   (b.) .

4
Level 6/Unit 1
Sentences: Statements and Questions

Extension: You may wish to have children describe a scary experience they have had and ask each other questions about it.

5

Macmillan/McGraw-Hill

COMMAND OR EXCLAMATION?

Call 9 1 1.
This is a command.

The house is burning!
This is an exclamation.

Read each sentence. Decide whether each sentence is a command or an exclamation. Put a period or an exclamation point at the end.

I. The dam broke_____

2. Tell us what happened_____

3. Don't step on the cat_____

4. Please clean your shoes_____

5. Find out the score_____

6. We won the game_____

7. Draw a picture for me_____

8. What a great picture_____

9. Please walk the dog_____

10. I love your new bike_____

Extension: You may wish to have the children write sentences about an exciting experience.

Level 6/Unit 1   10

Macmillan/McGraw-Hill

COMMAND SENTENCES

Remember

• A command is a sentence that tells or asks someone to do something.

• It ends with a period.

Start packing for vacation.   Get into the van.

Circle each command sentence.

1. Read the map.   2. Please start the van.

3. Drive carefully, Dad.   4. Head for the lake.

5. Trees grow along the way.   6. Are we almost there?

7. We have one hour to go.   8. Please turn on the radio.

9. At last, we are at the beach.   10. Help unload the van.

---

10 Level 6/Unit 1

Extension: You may wish to have the children take turns giving each other silly commands to follow.

EXCLAMATORY SENTENCES

Remember

- An exclamation is a sentence that shows strong feeling.
- It ends with an exclamation mark.

Mom won!

She got a prize!

Which of the sentences below are exclamatory? Find them and change the periods to exclamation points.

1. Mom is a good swimmer .

2. She entered a race .

3. The race started in the afternoon .

4. Then she took off like a rocket .

5. I wonder if the water is very chilly .

6. Hey look, that woman is passing her .

7. Hurry up, Mom .

8. She kept the lead .

9. We are so happy .

10. Mom is probably very tired .

Extension: You may wish to have the children give an excited account of an athletic event they watched or took part in.

Macmillan/McGraw-Hill

HOW DO YOU END THIS SENTENCE?

> ### Remember
>
> • A command ends with a period.
> • An exclamation ends with an exclamation mark.
>
> Help lift the dog, please.   The dog is so heavy!

Read this story.

The Dog Race

Rosie and her dad enter dog sled races. They race over miles of ice and snow. Sometimes the sled turns over. Then the dogs get tangled.

Choose the right mark to put after each sentence.
Fill in the circle next to the answer.

1. Please help harness the dogs together _____

   (a.) .
   (b.) !

2. Keep the reins loose in your hands _____

   (a.) .
   (b.) !

3. The lead dog is going much too fast _____

   (a.) .
   (b.) !

4. The sled is going to crash into that snowbank _____

   (a.) .
   (b.) !

4 Level 6/Unit 1
Command and Exclamatory Sentences:
End Punctuation

Extension: Have children act out a sled race using commands and exclamations to narrate the story.

9

WHAT ARE YOU AFRAID OF?

> **Remember**
>
> • A command tells or asks someone to do something.
> • An exclamation shows strong feeling.
>
> I can't see anything at all!   Please hand me the flashlight.
>
>

Read the beginning of the story. Then write the rest of the story yourself, using command and exclamatory sentences. Be sure to write at least four sentences.

Luke and Sarah are park rangers. They found the entrance to an underground cave. They peered into the dark hole. They could not see anything inside.

_____

_____

_____

_____

_____

_____

_____

Extension: Have children take turns telling about scary experiences, using exclamatory sentences.   Level 6/Unit 1   4

Macmillan/McGraw-Hill

CUTTING SENTENCES IN TWO

Subject   Predicate
My aunt | made a coat.

The coat | was too small.

She | gave the coat to me.

Then I | made a hat for her.

Draw a line between the subject and the predicate of each sentence.

1. Carrie needs a ride home.

2. She runs for the bus.

3. The bus drives away.

4. She looks for a friend.

5. Her friends took the first bus.

6. Carrie waits for the next bus.

7. Rosa comes and stands beside her.

8. The two girls start talking.

9. The next bus comes along.

10. The girls climb on the bus together.

Macmillan/McGraw-Hill

10

Level 6/Unit 1
Subjects and Predicates

Extension: You may wish to have children take turns starting
sentences for each other to finish.

11

SUBJECTS OF SENTENCES

Remember

- The **subject** of a sentence tells who or what does or did something.

Who opened the gate?

<u>The cat</u> opened the gate.

Which sentence tells about the picture? Draw a line under the subject of that sentence.

1.

     a. The mother opens the gate.

     b. The black dog opens the gate.

2.

     a. The gate is open.

     b. The spotted dog opens the gate.

3.

     a. The cat got out of the yard.

     b. The small black dog got out.

4.

     a. A strong wind carries the dog.

     b. The man carries the dog.

Extension: You may wish to have children write sentences to extend the story, using new subjects.

Macmillan/McGraw-Hill

PREDICATES OF SENTENCES

Remember

- The **predicate** of a sentence tells what the subject does or did.

  What does Grandpa do with the peas?

  Grandpa <u>plants the peas</u>.

Which sentence tells about the picture? Draw a line under the predicate of that sentence.

1.

   a. Grandpa digs in the garden.

   b. Grandpa drives his car.

2.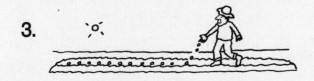

   a. Grandpa has an old snow shovel.

   b. Grandpa rakes the garden.

3.

   a. Grandpa eats peas and carrots.

   b. Grandpa plants the peas.

4.

   a. Grandpa picks the peas.

   b. Grandpa waters the peas.

Extension: You may wish to have children write sentences to extend the story using new predicates.

Macmillan/McGraw-Hill

WHAT IS MISSING?

> **Remember**
>
> - Every sentence has two parts.
> - The subject tells who or what does or did something.
> - The predicate tells what the subject does or did.

Read the story. Then read the words. Decide what is missing from each sentence. Fill in the circle by the answer.

Ben finds lots of cloth to make a quilt.
Then, he irons the cloth and cuts small pieces.
He lays the pieces carefully on the table.
Ben slowly begins to sew the pieces together.

1. Ben _____.

   ⓐ missing subject

   ⓑ missing predicate

2. _____ sews a yellow piece to a red piece.

   ⓐ missing subject

   ⓑ missing predicate

3. The colorful quilt _____.

   ⓐ missing subject

   ⓑ missing predicate

4. _____ finishes the quilt.

   ⓐ missing subject

   ⓑ missing predicate

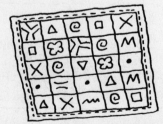

Macmillan/McGraw-Hill

Extension: You may wish to have children divide written sentences between the subject and the predicate, identify each part, and mix and match sentence parts to create new sentences.

HELLO TO GRANDMA

Remember

- Every sentence has two parts.
- The subject tells who or what does or did something.
- The predicate tells what the subject does or did.

My grandma lives in Mexico.   My grandma lives in Japan.

My grandma lives in Mexico.

My grandma lives in Japan.

Write a letter to someone in your family. Write two sentences about something you made or something you did.

Dear _____

_____

_____

_____

_____

Love,

_____

2
Level 6/Unit 1
Writing Subjects and Predicates

Extension: You may wish to have children use complete sentences to tell where their relatives live.

15

Macmillan/McGraw-Hill

MAKING LONGER SENTENCES

Jordan and Willy | are playing tennis at the park.

Jordan's uncle and aunt | ask if they can play.

The boys | are running and hitting the ball very fast.

The adults | go to play their own game.

Draw a line between the subject and the predicate of each sentence.

1. Paul looks at the rain and decides to stay inside.

2. He phones Kara and asks her to come over.

3. Paul and Kara play checkers and eat a snack.

4. Kara wins the first game and loses the second game.

5. Next, Kara and Paul play chess and then go outside.

Extension: You may wish to have children cut written sentences between the subject and the predicate, and then identify each part of the sentence.

Macmillan/McGraw-Hill

FINDING COMPOUND SUBJECTS

Remember

• The word **and** can be used to combine two subjects.
• The combination is called a **compound subject**.

Wilma plays the flute.   Nat plays the flute.

Wilma **and** Nat play the flute.

Which sentence tells about the picture? Fill in the circle next to the answer. Draw a line under the compound subject.

1.

    ⓐ Ted and Sally play ball.
    ⓑ Sally's brother plays ball.

2.

    ⓐ My pets are sleeping.
    ⓑ The lizard and the cat are not friends.

3.

    ⓐ My parents like to read.
    ⓑ My mom and dad dance.

4.

    ⓐ The three girls read.
    ⓑ Tina, Tanya, and Jill have lunch.

 Level 6/Unit 1

Extension: You may wish to have children take turns suggesting a compound subject for others to use in a complete sentence.

Macmillan/McGraw-Hill

FINDING COMPOUND PREDICATES

Remember

- The word **and** can be used to combine two predicates.
- The combination is called a **compound predicate**.

Max plays soccer.   Max studies music.

 Max plays soccer **and** studies music.

Which sentence tells about the picture? Fill in the circle next to the answer. Draw a line under the compound predicate.

1.

   (a.) The girl laughs out loud.
   (b.) The girl smiles and waves.

2.

   (a.) The boy swims and holds on.
   (b.) The boy blows bubbles.

3.

   (a.) The man sits and waits.
   (b.) The man sips his drink.

4.

   (a.) The girl watches the game.
   (b.) The girl kicks and runs.

Extension: You may wish to have children write a poem about a family celebration, using compound predicates.

COMPOUND SUBJECTS AND PREDICATES

Remember

- Two subjects can be combined, using **and.**
- Two predicates can be combined, using **and.**

Read the story. Draw a circle around the compound subjects.
Draw a line under the compound predicates.

1. George and Teddy plan to make a cake.

2. They find a bowl and break the eggs.

3. Then they put sugar into the eggs and beat the batter.

4. George and Teddy put the cake into the oven and bake it.

5. They watch the clock and wait until it is done.

6. They take the cake out and let it cool.

7. George and Teddy mix the frosting and put it on the cake.

8. Cake and ice cream will taste good after dinner.

Extension: You may wish to have children combine two sentences that
have the same subjects but different predicates.

Macmillan/McGraw-Hill

MIX AND MATCH

Remember

- Two subjects can be combined, using **and**.
- Two predicates can be combined, using **and**.

Look at the children and the things they can do. Choose any two children and any two things that they do. Make up one sentence using a **compound subject** and one sentence using a **compound predicate**.

Pam   Anna   Gina   Rose

Compound subject:

_____

Compound predicate:

_____

Extension: You may wish to have children continue making up sentences from the pictures and writing the sentences on another piece of paper.

Macmillan/McGraw-Hill

WHERE ARE THE NOUNS?

These underlined words are **nouns.**
My <u>room</u> is always messy.
I keep my <u>toys</u> on the <u>floor</u>.
I keep my <u>clothes</u> on the <u>chair</u>.
I have <u>animals</u> all over the <u>bed</u>.
There is <u>room</u> for only one more <u>thing</u>—me.

Read the sentences. Underline the nouns.

1. Two boys are planning a party for a friend.

2. Bill goes to the store to buy food and decorations.

3. Jeff buys juice, pretzels, apples, and balloons.

4. Jeff carries the supplies in one big bag.

5. The party will start this afternoon.

Extension: Have children name all the things they are wearing or carrying in a book bag.

WHICH NOUNS ARE PEOPLE?

> ## Remember
>
> • Some nouns name people.
>
>  man   child

Choose the noun that names a person.
Circle the letter next to it.

1. a. stone
    b. sister
    c. bike

2. a. doctor
    b. book
    c. telephone

3. a. airplane
    b. pilot
    c. cloud

4. a. uncle
    b. chair
    c. nap

5. a. dentist
    b. teeth
    c. smile

6. a. library
    b. teacher
    c. computer

Extension: Have children name the people who do community jobs,
such as deliver mail and direct traffic.

WHICH NOUNS ARE PLACES?

Remember

- Some nouns name places.

beach

hilltop

Circle the letter next to the noun that names a place.

1. a. ticket
   b. window
   c. station

2. a. glasses
   b. office
   c. doctor

3. a. neighborhood
   b. sunshine
   c. flower

4. a. milk
   b. store
   c. dime

5. a. swing
   b. park
   c. grass

6. a. bottle
   b. scissors
   c. school

Macmillan/McGraw-Hill

6

Level 6/Unit 2

Extension: Have children make up riddles that describe places so other children can guess the place name.

23

WHICH NOUNS ARE THINGS?

Remember

- Some nouns name things.

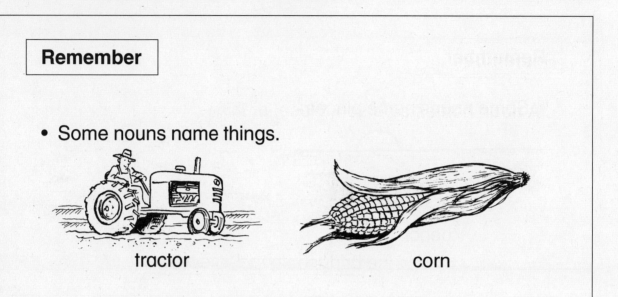

tractor   corn

Read the story. Circle the nouns that name things.

Alyssa gets out of bed before the sun comes up.

She looks out the window at the dark barn.

She puts on her jeans and shirt and jacket and glasses.

She goes out the door.

The cows are waiting in their stalls.

Alyssa sits on a stool.

One of the cows kicks over the bucket full of milk.

The cats and kittens lap up the milk.

Extension: Have children write a short story using three objects you name, such as a rope, a ladder, and a bird.

YOU TELL THE STORY

Remember

• A noun names a person, place, or thing.

The <u>giant</u> crossed the <u>bridge</u> into the little <u>town</u> .

Read the story. Fill in the blanks with nouns that name people, places, or things.

Roger awoke to hear a loud _____ . It was coming

from behind the _____ . He put on his

_____ and his _____ . Now he was

ready to find out what made the _____. He crept out of

the _____ . It was so dark he could not see anything.

Smash! Roger ran right into a _____ . He screamed.

"Don't worry," said his _____ who was standing right

next to him.

---

8 Level 6/Unit 2

Extension: Have children write their own stories without nouns, exchange papers, and fill in the blanks.

25

Name: _____   Date: _____

WHO'S THERE?

> The names of special people, places, and things begin with capital letters.
> My sister <u>Joan</u> has a cat named <u>Shep</u>.
> My friend <u>Bob</u> has a dog named <u>Sam</u>.

Read the sentences. Underline the nouns that name special people or animals.

1. Jenny and Todd are going to visit Tim.

2. On the way, they see Misha and Chuck with Jules.

3. Jules is a very, very small dog.

4. Misha can even carry Jules in his coat pocket.

5. Tim's dog is named Tiny.

6. Tiny is a very, very big dog.

7. The big dog barks and barks at Misha's coat pocket.

8. He can't see Jules, but he knows Jules is in the pocket.

9. Jules begins to bark.

10. Jenny, Misha, Chuck, and Tim all begin to laugh.

PEOPLE, PETS, AND PLACES

Remember
The names of special people, pets, and places begin with capital letters.

SPARKY

Henry and his dog Sparky live in Detroit.

Choose the proper noun in each group. Fill in the circle next to the correct answer.

1.
a. Molly
b. child
c. dancer

2.
a. planet
b. New York
c. big city

3.
a. airport
b. pilot
c. Ms. Emerson

4.
a. young writer
b. book award
c. Douglas Smith

5.
a. elephant
b. cow
c. Bessie

6.
a. Misty
b. kittens
c. basket

7.
a. gymnasium
b. library
c. Lincoln School

8.
a. fire station
b. newsstand
c. Tower Road

Extension: Have children take turns describing famous people or places. Have other children name the person or place being described.

27

DAYS, MONTHS, AND HOLIDAYS

Remember
• Nouns that name days, months, and holidays begin with capital letters.   <u>Halloween</u> is on <u>Thursday</u>,   the last day of <u>October.</u>

Choose the proper noun that names a day, month, or holiday.
Fill in the circle next to the correct answer.

1. (a.) celebration
   (b.) dinner
   (c.) Thanksgiving

2. (a.) Fourth of July
   (b.) summer
   (c.) parade

3. (a.) Monday
   (b.) tomorrow
   (c.) yesterday

4. (a.) football game
   (b.) Saturday
   (c.) flag raising

5. (a.) birthday
   (b.) springtime
   (c.) June

6. (a.) surprise test
   (b.) Tuesday
   (c.) Mrs. Jergens

7. (a.) January
   (b.) vacation
   (c.) travel

8. (a.) Presidents' Day
   (b.) assembly
   (c.) concert

Extension: Have children describe holiday celebrations that they celebrate with their families. Help them write the names of the holidays on the chalkboard.

8

STARTING OFF RIGHT

Remember

• A **proper noun** begins with a capital letter.

Ricardo and Louisa climbed Mount Rainier on Labor Day.

Look at the words under the pictures. Circle the word that is correct for each picture.

1.
Sally   sally

2.
runner   Runner

3.
barnaby   Barnaby

4.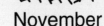
November   november

5.
babysitter   Babysitter

6.
anita   Anita

7.
Texas   texas

8.
Lawn mower   lawn mower

8   Level 6/Unit 2

Extension: Have one child name a word, and have the others stand up if the word should begin with a capital letter.

29

IN YOUR OWN WORDS

Remember
• A **proper noun** begins with a capital letter.

Read the sentences. Fill in each blank with a proper noun you choose from the lists in the chart.

HOLIDAYS	MONTHS	DAYS	PEOPLE	PLACES
Memorial Day July Fourth Labor Day Veterans' Day	November May October April	Tuesday Sunday Wednesday Thursday	Ron Caroline Rosita Leo	California Florida Maine Minnesota

I live in _____. On _____

I went to the amusement park. The park was filled with people. I

wondered why. Then I realized it was _____.

I met people from _____, _____, and

_____. More people kept coming. Then I saw

my friends _____ and _____.

Together we rode on the roller coaster and water slides. We made

plans to meet at the park next _____ or

_____. I can't wait to go back!

30

Extension: Have children make lists of proper nouns like those they used in the exercise, using names of their own friends and favorite holidays.

Level 6/Unit 2

10

Macmillan/McGraw-Hill

More Than One

How many <u>kittens</u> do you see?   I see seven <u>kittens</u>!

Circle the word that names each picture.

1.

ring   rings

2.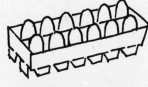

egg   eggs

3.

bats   bat

4.

flute   flutes

5.

helmet   helmets

6.

shoe   shoes

7.

rose   roses

8.

cars   car

Macmillan/McGraw-Hill

Extension: Have children give the plural form of objects you hold up,
pictures you show them, or words you call out.

Name: _____   Date: _____

NAMING MORE THAN ONE

Remember
- Add **s** to most nouns to name more than one.
- Add **es** to nouns that end with **s**, **ss**, **ch**, **sh**, and **x**.
    - One rock, but two rock**s**.
    - One box, but two box**es**.

Choose the right ending to make each word mean more than one.
Circle the correct answer.

1. watch

    a. watches

    b. watchs

2. cup

    a. cupes

    b. cups

3. spoon

    a. spoones

    b. spoons

4. guess

    a. guesses

    b. guesss

5. picture

    a. picturees

    b. pictures

6. zebra

    a. zebraes

    b. zebras

7. brush

    a. brushes

    b. brushs

8. lace

    a. lacees

    b. laces

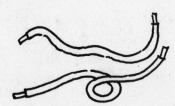

PLURAL NOUNS ENDING WITH Y

Remember

- If a word ends with a consonant and **y**, change **y** to **i** and add **es** to name more than one.

I have a new baby sister.   Pat has a new baby brother.

That makes two new bab**ies** on our block!

Read the first word in each row. Then circle the word that means more than one.

1. **candy**   candies   cande   candi

2. **lily**   lilys   lilie   lilies

3. **mommy**   mommie   mommies   mommys

4. **daddy**   daddies   daddys   daddes

5. **poppy**   poppis   poppies   popps

6. **story**   storis   storys   stories

7. **daisy**   daises   daseys   daisies

8. **family**   familys   familey   families

Extension: Have children suggest other nouns that end with *y* and write the plural form of each one.

OTHER KINDS OF PLURAL NOUNS

> Remember
> - Some nouns change their spelling to name more than one.
>
> One **mouse** sneaks into the house.
> Along come two more **mice**.

Look at the words under each picture. Circle the word that means more than one.

1.

child   children

2.

men   man

3.

woman   women

4.

teeth   tooth

5.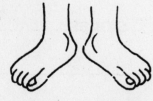

feet   foot

6.

goose   geese

Macmillan/McGraw-Hill

TWO OF EVERYTHING

Remember

- Add **s** to most nouns to name more than one.
- Add **es** to nouns that end with **s**, **ss**, **ch**, **sh**, and **x**.
- If a word ends with a consonant and **y**, change **y** to **i** and add **es** to name more than one.
- Some nouns change their spelling to name more than one.

Write a story about twins. Use two of everything in your story. Use at least five words from the box in your story.

twins	feet	boxes	candies	shoes	guesses

_____

_____

_____

_____

_____

_____

_____

_____

_____

Extension: Have children name parts of their bodies, first using the singular and then using the plural form.

Macmillan/McGraw-Hill

POSSESSIVE NOUNS

Does the ball belong to Joy?   Yes, it is Joy's ball.

Does this mitt belong to Dad?   Yes, it is Dad's mitt.

Complete the phrase that names each picture. Use the words from the box.

| Jason's | visitor's | dragon's | doctor's | horse's | astronaut's |

1.

the _____ suit

2.

the _____ fish

3.

the _____ hay

4.

the _____ suitcase

5.

the _____ patient

6.

_____ trophy

Extension: Have children give the possessive form of objects you hold up, pictures you show them, or words you call out.

Level 6/Unit 2   6

SHOWING POSSESSION

| Remember |

- Add an apostrophe and **s** to show that someone owns something.

The watch belongs to the nurse.

It is the nurse**'s** watch.

Choose the right word to fill each blank. Circle your answer.

1. _____ nose
   a. Paul's
   b. Paul

2. _____ smile
   a. Kate's
   b. Kate

3. _____ feet
   a. babys
   b. baby's

4. _____ hands
   a. Marc
   b. Marc's

5. _____ hair
   a. Moms
   b. Mom's

6. _____ knees
   a. Claire's
   b. Claires

7. _____ teeth
   a. Jamies
   b. Jamie's

8. _____ eyes
   a. reader's
   b. reader

Extension: Have children describe something a classmate owns using the possessive form of the name.

POSSESSIVES FOR WORDS ENDING IN S

| Remember |

• Add an apostrophe to a plural noun that ends in **s** to show that more than one own something.

The sister**s'** turtles escaped from the bowl.
The boy**s'** dinners were getting cold.

Read the words in the first column. Circle the word that shows the correct way to show that more than one own something.

1. scouts tents	scout's	scouts'	scout
2. pilots hats	pilots	pilots'	pilot's
3. puppies ears	puppies'	puppies	puppy's
4. books covers	books	books'	books's
5. monkeys tails	monkey's	monkies	monkeys'
6. dancers arms	dancers'	dancers	dancer's
7. birds beaks	bird's	birds'	birds
8. singers voices	singers	singers'	singer's
9. actors costumes	actor's	actors	actors'
10. nurses shoes	nurses	nurses'	nurses'es

Extension: Have children write the correct possessive form of other plural words.

Level 6/Unit 2

10

USING POSSESSIVE EN[...]

> **Remember**
> • If a noun names one, add a[...]
> someone owns something.
> • If a noun names more than [...]
> to show that someone owns so[...]
> Jack**'s** mother**'s** father is Ja[...]

Circle the word that finishes the se[...]

1. The water made the _____
   cover fall off.

2. The _____ boxes were
   different sizes.

3. The wind made all the _____
   speeds change.

4. The _____ horns stood up on   cov[...]
   its head.

5. My _____ wheels hummed.   bicycle'[...]

6. Different names were printed   flower's

   on the _____ boxes.

Macmillan/McGraw-Hill

Extension: Have children create long lists of linked possessive v[...]
(baby's rattle's handle's color, etc.) .

n that names one to show

un that ends in **s** to show that

to visit. Her friends' children are

hat you might find in Rosita's locked
at someone owns something in your
s from the box in your story.

sides'	key's	lock's	friends'

_____

_____

_____

_____

_____

_____

_____

_____

n: Have children name an object, and have others tell whose it
g the possessive form of the name or noun.

Level 6/Unit 2

 4

ACTION VERBS

An action verb shows action.

Kevin <u>hits</u> the ball into the air.
He <u>runs</u> to first base.
Makiko <u>catches</u> the ball and <u>runs</u> to second base.

Circle the words that show action in each sentence.

1. Martin dresses in shorts and a t-shirt.

2. His mother drives him to the starting point.

3. He kisses his mother and gets out of the car.

4. He lines up with the other runners.

5. BANG! The pistol goes off.

6. The runners push off.

7. Martin moves his legs faster and faster.

8. He pumps his arms.

9. He speeds across the finish line.

10. Martin catches his breath at last and smiles at his mom.

Macmillan/McGraw-Hill

WHERE'S THE ACTION?

Remember
- An **action verb** is a word that shows action.

Ravi and Katie <u>bake</u> a pizza.
They <u>make</u> lemonade.
Then they <u>call</u> their friends.
The friends <u>come</u> to Katie's house.
They <u>eat</u> the pizza and <u>drink</u> the lemonade.

Circle the action word that goes with each picture.

1. a. dance
   b. dancer
   c. fly

2. a. street
   b. swim
   c. ride

3. a. plane
   b. fly
   c. spin
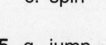

4. a. read
   b. magazine
   c. sleep

5. a. jump
   b. leg
   c. walk

6. a. upstairs
   b. sit
   c. carry

7. a. pull
   b. push
   c. sidewalk

8. a. wash
   b. car
   c. dry

Extension: Have children describe the actions of their favorite animals
or pets using action verbs.

Macmillan/McGraw-Hill

USING ACTION VERBS

| Remember |

      • An action verb is a word that shows action.

      Louis often <u>goes</u> home for lunch.
      Every Friday he <u>eats</u> with his friends.

Underline the action verbs. Then write the verbs on the lines.

1. A mouse looks up.   _____

2. He sees a giant hand.   _____

3. The hand reaches for the mouse.   _____

4. The hand lifts the mouse.   _____

5. The mouse squeaks.   _____

6. The mouse wiggles.   _____

7. The hand drops the mouse.   _____

8. The mouse lands on the floor.   _____

9. He runs across the floor and into his hole. _____

10. He plans his next trip to the kitchen.   _____

Now use the space below to draw a picture to show what happened in one of the sentences above.

Extension: Have children draw a cartoon strip and label it with action verbs.

USING MORE ACTION VERBS

> **Remember**
> • An action verb is a word that shows action.
>
> Zack and Greg <u>slide</u> down the hill.
> They <u>speed</u> over the snow.

Fill in each blank with an action verb from the box. You can use a word more than once.

1. _____ down the street

2. _____ over the hill

3. _____ the cow

4. _____ into the room

5. _____ the sign

6. _____ the directions

7. _____ very fast

8. _____ the gate

run
swim
sneak
follow
climb
read
open

Extension: Have children create sentences with blanks where action verbs belong, and have other children fill them in.

Macmillan/McGraw-Hill

WARREN'S LOST HAMSTER

Remember
 • An action verb is a word that shows action.

Karen <u>walks</u> her dog twice a day.
She <u>feeds</u> him biscuits.
She <u>brushes</u> his coat.

Write a story about Warren's lost pet. Describe the hamster. Tell what he does. Tell what Warren is doing to find him. Circle five action verbs you used.

One day, Warren's hamster
wandered out of his cage ....

_____

_____

_____

_____

_____

_____

_____

Macmillan/McGraw-Hill

PRESENT-TENSE VERBS

> Maggie **goes** to the fabric store.
> She **buys** some fabric.
> She **sews** a costume for herself.
>
> The words **goes**, **buys**, and **sews** are present-tense verbs.

Underline the words that show action in the present tense.

1. The skunk wakes up early in the morning.

2. He shivers in the cold air.

3. He searches for food.

4. The skunk finds a few nuts to eat.

5. Then he finds some people's garbage.

6. He digs in the garbage and scatters it around.

7. He sees an apple and some bread.

8. He eats the food.

9. The skunk yawns.

10. He returns to his home and takes a nap.

Extension: Have children tell stories about animals who live in the wilderness, using present-tense verbs.

Level 6/Unit 3

12

FORMING SINGULAR VERBS

Remember

- Some verbs tell about actions that happen now.
- Add **s** to most verbs to tell what one person or thing does now.

Thomas <u>write**s**</u> a poem.   Anna <u>read**s**</u> the poem out loud.

Circle the word that tells what one person does now.

1. a. tell
   b. tells

2. a. walk
   b. walks

3. a. knows
   b. know

4. a. taps
   b. tap

5. a. see
   b. sees

6. a. spins
   b. spin

7. a. says
   b. say

8. a. save
   b. saves

9. a. ride
   b. rides

10. a. hugs
    b. hug

11. a. talk
    b. talks

12. a. laughs
    b. laugh

Extension: Have children describe a series of actions in the present tense, using the verbs on the page.

RECOGNIZING PLURAL VERBS

| Remember |

• Do **not** add **s** to verbs that tell what more than one person or thing does now.

The puppies <u>snuggle</u> together.
Their ears <u>stand</u> up.
Their tails <u>wag</u>.

Circle the words that tell what more than one person does now.

1. Drew and Peter find a shiny coin.

2. They take it home to show their parents.

3. Their parents drive them to a coin store.

4. The boys show the coin to the coin dealer.

5. The coins in the showcase sparkle.

6. Peter and Drew notice a coin like theirs.

7. They ask the man if it is the same.

8. They hope their coin is worth a lot of money.

Macmillan/McGraw-Hill

Extension: Have children work in pairs to pantomime actions for other children to describe, using plural present tense verbs.

8

PRESENT-TENSE VERBS FOR I OR YOU

> **Remember**
> • Do **not** add **s** to the verb if the subject is **I** or **you**.
>   **I play** chess. **Do you?**
>   **You play** chess better than **I do!**

Underline the verbs that tell what **I** or **you** do now. Then write the verbs on the lines.

You take the seeds out of the packet.   1. _____

I make a hole in the ground.   2. _____

You count three seeds.   3. _____

You hand the seeds to me.   4. _____

I plant the seeds in the hole.   5. _____

Then I dig another hole nearby.   6. _____

You count three more seeds.   7. _____

You kneel down and place the   8. _____
seeds in the ground.
                                                 9. _____

I get the watering can.   10. _____

Extension: Have children create dialogues in which they use present-tense verbs with *I* or *you*.

WRITING DESCRIPTIONS

| Remember |

- Some verbs tell about actions that happen now.
- Add **s** to most verbs to tell what one person or thing does now.
- Do **not** add s to verbs that tell what more than one person or thing does now.
- Do **not** add s if the subject is *I* or *you*.

Write a description of a movie or television show. Tell what happens in the show using the present tense. Write at least five sentences.

_____

_____

_____

_____

_____

PAST-TENSE VERBS

What **happened** at the party?
Frances **opened** her presents and we all **sang** Happy Birthday.

Circle the words that show action in the past tense.

1. Chester climbed the steps to the top of the slide.

2. He stood a long time and looked out.

3. He shivered because he was cold.

4. The slide gleamed in the sun.

5. The other children called to Chester to come down.

6. Finally, he decided to go down.

7. He sat on the very top.

8. Then he shoved off suddenly.

9. Swoosh! He slid all the way to the bottom.

10. He splashed into the water and came up laughing.

Macmillan/McGraw-Hill

12 Level 6/Unit 3

Extension: Have children tell what they did after school yesterday, using verbs in the past tense.

RECOGNIZING THE PAST TENSE

Remember

• Verbs can tell about actions that happened in the past.

Erika **walked** to the bread store.
Erika **looked** at the loaves of bread.
Erika **tasted** one loaf.

Circle the past-tense verb.

1. a. enjoy
   b. enjoyed

2. a. lifted
   b. lift

3. a. asked
   b. ask

4. a. turn
   b. turned

5. a. learned
   b. learn

6. a. talk
   b. talked

7. a. guess
   b. guessed

8. a. bake
   b. baked

9. a. rested
   b. rest

10. a. folded
    b. fold

Extension: Have children write sentences, using five of the past-tense verbs they circled in the exercise.

Level 6/Unit 3

10

Macmillan/McGraw-Hill

FORMING PAST-TENSE VERBS

| Remember |

- Add **ed** to most verbs to tell about actions that happened in the past.

The dinosaurs roar.	The dinosaurs roar**ed**.
They stamp their feet.	They stamp**ed** their feet.
The trees shiver.	The trees shiver**ed**.

Find the underlined present-tense verbs. Then write each verb in the past tense.

The big animals <u>stalk</u> the little ones. 1. _____

They <u>follow</u> them everywhere. 2. _____

The little animals <u>open</u> their eyes wide. 3. _____

They <u>call</u> to each other. 4. _____

The other animals <u>listen</u>. 5. _____

They <u>jump</u> and <u>climb</u> into trees. 6. _____

7. _____

They <u>leap</u> over the streams. 8. _____

The big animals <u>roar</u>. 9. _____

The little animals <u>squeak</u>. 10. _____

Extension: Have children write new sentences, using the past-tense verbs in the exercise.

FORMING PAST-TENSE VERBS

<table>
<tr><td>

Remember

- Add **d** to some verbs to tell about actions in the past.

We rake the leaves.   We rake**d** the leaves.

</td></tr>
</table>

Find the underlined present-tense verbs. Then write each verb in the past tense.

1. Felina and Faith <u>bake</u> a pie. _____

2. They <u>pare</u> the apples. _____

3. They <u>poke</u> holes in the crust. _____

4. They <u>handle</u> the pie very carefully. _____

5. They <u>grate</u> cheese over the top. _____

6. Faith and Felina <u>move</u> the pie to the table. _____

7. They <u>place</u> it on a plate. _____

8. Then they <u>slice</u> the pie. _____

Extension: Have children pantomime the story in the exercise while others call out the verbs.

WRITING A NEWS STORY

Remember

- Verbs can tell about actions that happened in the past.
- Add **ed** to most verbs to tell about actions in the past.
- Add **d** to some verbs to tell about actions in the past.

  Rachel glue**d** the red heart to the white paper.
  She mail**ed** the valentine.

Write a news story. Tell about something that happened last night.
Make it sound exciting. Use at least five past-tense verbs.

_____

_____

_____

_____

_____

_____

5 | Level 6/Unit 3

Extension: Have children exchange stories and circle the past-tense verbs.

55

HAS OR HAVE?

Benita **has** a book. Chad also **has** a book.
Benita and Chad both **have** books.

Read each sentence. Choose **has** or **have** to complete each sentence. Circle the letter next to the correct answer.

I. Nick and Carol _____ ten dollars.
   a. has
   b. have

2. Dwayne _____ four dollars.
   a. has
   b. have

3. Ted _____ five dollars.
   a. has
   b. have

4. Ted _____ a plan.
   a. has
   b. have

5. They _____ enough money for a movie.
   a. has
   b. have

6. They do not _____ enough money for popcorn.
   a. has
   b. have

7. Ted _____ some popcorn already.
   a. has
   b. have

8. They always _____ a very good time at the movies.
   a. has
   b. have

Macmillan/McGraw-Hill

WHAT WORDS GO WITH HAS?

Remember

- Use **has** to tell about one person or thing.

  Cherry **has** a purple fish.
  Cherry's fish **has** a yellow fin.
  The yellow fin **has** a green stripe.
  The green stripe **has** a pink dot.

Read the sentences. Look at the words in the box. Choose a word to complete each sentence. Write the word in the blank.

tank	fish	net	snail
room	shirt	turtle	cat

1. Taylor's _____ has four walls.

2. His _____ has four fish in it.

3. His _____ has blue eyes.

4. His _____ has two little eyes.

5. His _____ has tiny holes in it.

6. His _____ has purple stripes.

7. His _____ has sharp claws.

8. His _____ has yellow dots.

Extension: Have children create other sentences to be completed with words from the box.

Macmillan/McGraw-Hill

WHAT WORDS GO WITH HAVE?

> **Remember**
>
> • Use **have** to tell about more than one.
>
> Melvin and Jerry **have** everything they need to go fishing.
> Will they **have** good luck?

Read the sentences. Circle the word that belongs in each sentence.

1. Melvin and Jerry **has have** time before breakfast.

2. They **has have** enough bait to go fishing.

3. Tanya **has have** a boat.

4. They **has have** fishing rods for everyone.

5. The children **has have** fun waiting for the fish to bite.

6. They **has have** time to catch many fish for breakfast.

7. Their parents **has have** the pan ready to fry the fish.

8. They **has have** a very good time eating breakfast.

9. They all **has have** more fish than they can eat.

10. They even **has have** enough to take home.

Extension: Have children stand in front of the class by twos and have other children describe something the two have in common, using the word *have*.

10

MORE USES FOR HAVE

| Remember |

- Use **have** if the subject is **I** or **you**.
  You **have** a big smile on your face.
  I **have** some good news!

You have a big smile on your face.

I have some good news!

Read the sentences. Fill in the blanks with **have** or **has**.

1. Tad _____ two missing teeth.

2. You _____ three missing teeth.

3. I _____ one missing tooth.

4. Do you _____ any new teeth?

5. Sylvie _____ braces on her teeth.

6. I do not _____ braces on my teeth.

7. I _____ two new teeth.

8. What kind of toothbrush do you _____?

9. I _____ one that glows in the dark.

10. Corky _____ a toothbrush like mine.

Macmillan/McGraw-Hill

10 Level 6/Unit 3

Extension: Have children take turns asking and telling each other about their missing teeth.

59

MYSTERY SENTENCES WITH HAVE AND HAS

Our hill **has** seven houses.
Our house **has** seven rooms.
I **have** seven animals on my bed.
You **have** seven animals, too.

Grace found a story torn into pieces. She is trying to put the pieces together. Draw lines to connect the two parts of each sentence. You can use the same ending more than once.

1. Lonely Zeke   has no friends to play with.

2. He   have time to call Zeke.

3. Zeke's friends all   has books to read, too.

4. For once Zeke   has books to read.

5. He   has nothing to do after school.

6. Paula   have somewhere to go.

7. Even on the weekend she   has something to do today.

8. Maybe this weekend Paula   has a lot of homework, too.
   will
                                 have a lot to talk about.
9. Zeke
                                 has a lot of homework.
10. Paula and Zeke

Extension: Have children take turns starting sentences which others must finish using phrases that start with *have* or *has*.

Level 6/Unit 3   10

Macmillan/McGraw-Hill

FINDING HELPING VERBS

Carrie **has** cut the bushes.
The boys **have** mowed the lawn.
Everyone **has** done a great job.

Read the story. Circle the helping verbs.

1. Paula has practiced her part in the drama club play.

2. She has learned her lines.

3. Jim and Floyd have teased her.

4. They have not learned their lines yet.

5. Opening night has arrived.

6. The curtain has risen.

7. Paula has finished her part.

8. Jim and Floyd have come on stage.

8 Level 7/Unit 1

Extension: Have children act out a baseball game while others describe
the action using helping verbs *has* and *have*.

61

USING HAVE AS A HELPING VERB

Remember

- A helping verb helps to show an action.
- **Have** is used with plural subjects, and **I** or **you**.

The runners **have** all crossed the finish line.
I **have** come in second.
You **have** come in first.

Read each sentence. Circle the picture that goes with the sentence.

1. Pete and Will have eaten dinner.

2. They have put on pajamas.

3. They have climbed into their beds.

4. They have fallen asleep.

Extension: Have children continue the story of Pete and Will, telling about what they *have done* the next morning.

Level 7/Unit 1

4

Macmillan/McGraw-Hill

USING HAS AS A HELPING VERB

Remember

- A helping verb helps to show an action.
- **Has** is used with singular subjects.

  Nona **has** eaten two peaches.
  Sara **has** eaten only one.

Read the sentences. Circle the word that belongs in each sentence.

1. Jenny **has** **have** found a silver dollar.

2. She **has** **have** shown it to her friend Lou.

3. Lou and Jenny **has** **have** looked around for more coins.

4. They **has** **have** found three more.

5. Lou **has** **have** put up a sign telling about the lost coins.

6. Mr. Garret **has** **have** read the sign.

7. He **has** **have** called Lou on the telephone.

8. He **has** **have** come to see the coins.

9. Mr. Garret **has** **have** said the coins are not his.

10. Lou and Jenny **has** **have** put the coins in a safe place.

Extension: Have children describe what has happened to a character in a television show or a movie, using *has* as a helping verb.

USING HAD AS A HELPING VERB

| Remember |

- A helping verb helps to show an action.
- **Had** is used with all subjects to show action in the past.

Gordon went skiing in the mountains.
He **had** skied once before.
He **had** not learned how to turn very well.

Read the sentences. Circle the answer with the helping verb.

I. Gordon   had taken   one skiing lesson.
                  took

2. He   climbed   to the top of the hill.
         had climbed

3. We   waved   to Gordon from the bottom.
         had waved

4. I   had told   Gordon to come down the hill.
         told

5. Gordon   had stood   at the top for a long time.
               stood

6. He   looked   all the way to the bottom.
         had looked

7. Gordon   had started   down the hill.
               started

8. Gordon   had reached   the bottom at last.
               reached

Macmillan/McGraw-Hill

USING HAVE, HAS, AND HAD

Remember

- A helping verb helps to show an action.
- **Have** is used with plural subjects and **I** or **you.**
- **Has** is used with singular subjects.
- **Had** is used with all subjects to show action in the past.

Read the sentences. Write a helping verb in the blank.
Choose **has, have,** or **had.**

1. I _____ written a letter to my mother.

2. She _____ written me a reply.

3. My father and I _____ called her on the telephone.

4. My mother and father _____ talked a long time.

5. My father _____ given me a bus ticket.

6. I _____ looked at the map.

7. My father and I _____ packed our suitcases.

8. My mother _____ found a place for us to stay.

9. I _____ gone to bed but not to sleep.

10. You _____ offered to drive us to the station.

Macmillan/McGraw-Hill

Extension: Have children use sentences with helping verbs to tell about
preparing to take a trip.

IRREGULAR VERBS

Angela **sees** a dog.	Angela **saw** a dog.
Angela **sings** a tune.	Angela **sang** a tune.

Read the sentences. How would you change each sentence to make it tell about the past? Choose the right word to replace the underlined verb. Circle your answer.

1. Patti <u>sees</u> a parade.
   a. seed
   b. saw

2. Patti <u>begins</u> to cross the street.
   a. beginned
   b. began

3. She <u>runs</u> the rest of the way.
   a. runned
   b. ran

4. Ted and Charlie <u>come</u> behind the band, juggling.
   a. comed
   b. came

5. I <u>give</u> you my program.
   a. gave
   b. gived

6. The parade <u>goes</u> to the end of the street.
   a. goed
   b. went

Extension: Have children write sentences in the present for others to convert to the past, using irregular verbs.

Level 7/Unit 1

6

Macmillan/McGraw-Hill

USING DO, SEE, AND COME

> **Remember**
> - Some verbs have special forms.
> - Some irregular verbs are **do, see,** and **come.**
>
>
>
> Some dogs **do** tricks.
> My dog **does** a lot of tricks.
> He **did** all his tricks for the visitors.

Read each sentence. Circle the form of the verb that belongs
in the sentence.

1. Randy   does   a cartwheel.
               do

2. He   seed   a bird on the ground.
               saw

3. The bird   came   to Randy.
               comed

4. We   sees   that the bird was hurt.
               saw

5. We all   came   closer.
               comes

6. The bird   do   not seem to mind.
               did

Extension: Have children create their own sentences with the irregular
verbs.

USING GO, RUN, AND GIVE

| Remember |

- Some verbs have special forms.
- Some irregular verbs are **go, run,** and **give**.

I **go** to karate lessons every Tuesday.
Ian **goes** on Wednesday.
I **went** last night.

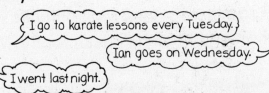

Read the sentences. Circle the correct form of the verb.

I. Rick **gave gived** Jody a trumpet lesson.

2. Jody **ran runned** to get there on time.

3. Rick **goes go** to band every Wednesday.

4. Walt and Pedro **goes go** to chorus every day.

5. They **ran runned** when they were late.

6. Rick and Jody **gave gived** me a ride.

7. I **go goes** to hockey in the winter.

8. We **ran runned** during the summer.

Extension: Have children use irregular forms of *go, run,* and *give* to retell a favorite story.

Macmillan/McGraw-Hill

USING BEGIN AND SING

> Remember
> - Some verbs have special forms.
> - Some irregular verbs are **begin** and **sing**.

Read the sentences. Fill in the blanks with one of the words in the word box.

begin	begins	began
sing	sings	sang

1. School _____ tomorrow.

2. Margo and Peter will _____ the same day.

3. Sometimes Peter _____ when he is nervous.

4. They always _____ a song when they are together.

5. We _____ this song long ago in nursery school.

6. The song _____ with the ABCs.

7. "Please don't _____ at the table," said Mother.

8. She _____ to go to school when she was six years old.

9. "Did you ever _____ this song?" I asked her.

10. We _____ that song just yesterday.

Extension: Have children make a chart showing all the irregular forms of the verbs *sing* and *begin*. Have them create sentences using varying forms of each verb.

69

Macmillan/McGraw-Hill

TELLING A STORY WITH IRREGULAR VERBS

- Some verbs have special forms.
- Some irregular verbs are **do, see, come, go, run, give, begin,** and **sing.**

Marcus **gave** the magic penny to the elf.
Now the elf **comes** whenever Marcus calls him.

Write a story about Marcus and the elf. Use at least four
of the irregular verbs shown in the box.

did	**saw**
came	**went**
ran	**gave**
began	**sang**

_____

_____

_____

_____

_____

_____

_____

Extension: Have children read their stories out loud and compile them
into a book for others to read.   Level 7/Unit 1   **4**

Macmillan/McGraw-Hill

RECOGNIZING LINKING VERBS

Tony **is** a dog.　　　　Tony **is** asleep.
Tony and Fluff **are** pets.　Tony and Fluff **are** sneaky.

Read the sentences. Choose the word that belongs in the blank.
Circle the correct answer.

1. Tony _____ bigger than I
   am.
   a. is
   b. are

2. Tony and Fluff _____ still
   puppies.
   a. is
   b. are

3. They _____ asleep right
   now.
   a. is
   b. are

4. I _____ ready for them to
   wake up.
   a. am
   b. are

5. Now Tony _____ awake.
   a. is
   b. are

6. Fluff _____ still curled up.
   a. is
   b. are

7. Fluff _____ suddenly
   awake, too.
   a. is
   b. am

8. Now the three of us
   _____ ready to play.
   a. is
   b. are

8

Level 7/Unit 1

Extension: Have children describe the locations of classroom objects
using *is* and *are*.

71

LINKING VERBS IN THE PRESENT AND PAST

| Remember |

- A linking verb connects the subject to the rest of the sentence.
- It does not show action.
- Linking verbs can tell about the present or the past.
- Some linking verbs are **is, seem, feel,** and **look**.

Marcia **seems** cranky.
She **seemed** all right last night.

Marcia seems cranky.
She seemed all right last night.

Read the sentences. Circle the linking verbs in the present.
Then write the linking verb in the past on the line.

Present   **Past**

1. The snow is very deep.   _____

2. The sun seems very bright.   _____

3. The snow looks wet.   _____

4. It seems softer than usual.   _____

5. It is good for making snowballs.   _____

6. The sun is behind a cloud.   _____

7. The snow feels harder.   _____

8. Jon is ready to build a snow fort.   _____

72

Extension: Have children write a descriptive poem using linking verbs
in the past and present.

Level 7/Unit 1   8

Macmillan/McGraw-Hill

LINKING VERBS FOR SINGULAR AND PLURAL

Remember

- A linking verb connects the subject to the rest of the sentence.
- It does not show action.
- Linking verbs can tell about singular and plural subjects.
- Some linking verbs are **is, seem, feel,** and **look**.
  Toby and Lenny **are** sick. Lenny **is** still in bed.
  Toby **is** reading quietly.

Read the sentences. Circle the correct form of the verb.

1. Lenny **feel feels** a little better today.

2. Toby and Lenny **look looks** better than they did yesterday.

3. Uncle Ron **is am** happy to see them getting better.

4. He **seem seems** to have an idea.

5. He will tell them the plan when Toby and Lenny **is are** well.

6. For now the plan **is am** a secret.

7. Toby **look looks** excited.

8. Does he **feel feels** good enough to go outside?

Extension: Have children use singular and plural forms of *is, seem, feel,* and *look* to describe the weather outside today.

USING LINKING VERBS

Remember

- A linking verb connects the subject to the rest of the sentence.
- It does not show action.
  These old bikes **are** rusty.
  Long ago the bikes **were** new.
  They **were** shiny then.

Read the sentences. Write a word from the word box that makes the sentence tell about the **present**. Then write the word you would use to make the sentence tell about the **past** in the past column.

am	was	are	were	is

Present   **Past**

1. The old garage _____ full of old bicycles.   _____

2. Tim and I _____ excited to find them.   _____

3. The bikes _____ rusty and bent.   _____

4. They _____ not ready to ride.   _____

5. Tim and I _____ ready to go to work.   _____

6. Tim _____ good at fixing things   _____

7. I _____ good at painting.   _____

8. Together we _____ able to fix all the bikes.   _____

Extension: Have children translate sentences you give them, which contain linking verbs, from present to past.

Level 7/Unit 1   8

Macmillan/McGraw-Hill

TELLING A STORY WITH LINKING VERBS

- A linking verb connects the subject to the rest of the sentence.
- It does not show action.

  Mandy **looks** puzzled.
  She **is** confused about the game.

Help Mandy by filling in the blanks in her story. For each blank, choose one of the linking verbs in the box. Then fill in the blank with the correct form of the verb.

seem	look	feel	am	was
seems	looks	feels	is	were
seemed	looked	felt	are	

Mandy _____ terribly grouchy this morning.

She _____ very tired. It _____ a shame that

she does not _____ very happy. Her parents _____

quite upset by her. They _____ not at all pleased.

Mandy _____ hungry for breakfast. Now she _____

full. Her friends _____ happy to see her. Now she

_____ better than ever. All she needed

was breakfast!

Macmillan/McGraw-Hill

Extension: Have children compare their stories and tell why they chose the verb forms they chose.

RECOGNIZING CONTRACTIONS

Read the story. Circle the contractions.

1. Willi won't get ready for the play.

2. He wants to stay home and watch television instead.

3. We didn't get a sitter for Willi.

4. So Willi has to come to the play.

5. He says he isn't going to like the play.

6. He says he can't hear the actors.

7. He says plays don't interest him.

8. We aren't going without him.

Extension: Have children make up dialogues in which one child refuses
to do something using *can't* and *won't* while the other insists.

Macmillan/McGraw-Hill

CANNOT = CAN'T

Remember

- A contraction is a short form of two words.
- An apostrophe takes the place of letters that are left out.

Lucy **cannot** finish her milk.
Lucy **can't** finish her milk.

Read each sentence. Write **can't** in the first blank. Then circle the answer to each riddle.

1. Grandpa _____ read without his _____.
   a. glasses **b.** brush
   c. shoes

2. Jenny _____ write without her _____.
   a. carrot **b.** pen **c.** hat

3. Ted _____ walk in the rain without his _____.
   a. apple **b.** umbrella **c.** car

4. The dog _____ eat his dinner without his _____.
   a. fork **b.** spoon **c.** bowl

5. A bird _____ fly without its _____.
   a. beak **b.** wings **c.** feet

6. A fish _____ breathe without its _____.
   a. gills **b.** eyes **c.** mouth

12 Level 7/Unit 1
Contractions: *can't*

Extension: Have children describe a difficult situation using contractions in the lesson.

77

Macmillan/McGraw-Hill

DID NOT = DIDN'T

> Remember
>
> - A contraction is a short form of two words.
>
> - An apostrophe takes the place of letters that are left out.
>
>   Lucy **did not** eat lunch.
>   Lucy **didn't** eat lunch.

Read the sentences. Circle the correct contraction to complete each sentence.

1. I   didn't   put my slippers under the bed.
           di'dnt

2. Nathan   didn't   borrow my slippers.
              dint'

3. Nathan   ca'nt   wear my size.
              can't

4. I   didnot   take them off.
           didn't

5. The cat   can't   wear my slippers.
              cant'

6. They   diddnt   run away by themselves.
            didn't

Macmillan/McGraw-Hill

Extension: Have children describe a search for something that is missing using the contractions in the lesson.

DO NOT = DON'T

> **Remember**
> - A contraction is a short form of two words.
> - An apostrophe takes the place of letters that are left out.
>
>   I **do not** want to go shopping.
>   I **don't** know what to buy.

Write the contraction for the underlined words in each sentence.

1. I <u>do not</u> like to keep secrets from Mom. _____

2. But Mom <u>cannot</u> know about her party. _____

3. Dad <u>did not</u> tell her because it's a surprise. _____

4. I <u>did not</u> buy a present yet. _____

5. I <u>do not</u> have much money to spend. _____

6. I <u>cannot</u> buy fancy earrings. _____

7. And I <u>do not</u> like to buy clothes. _____

8. I <u>cannot</u> think of what to buy. _____

8 Level 7/Unit 1
Contractions: *don't*

Extension: Have children tell a mystery story using the contractions from this lesson.

79

Macmillan/McGraw-Hill

USING CONTRACTIONS

Remember
• A contraction is a short form of two words.
• An apostrophe takes the place of letters that are left out.

Read the sentences. Complete each sentence with a contraction from the box.

can't	didn't	don't

I _____ like rainy weekends. When it rains, I _____ go outside. We _____ go to the beach yesterday. And we _____ go for a picnic today. I _____ want to stay inside. I _____ think of anything to do. Wait! _____ I see a copy of *The Secret Garden* on my sister's bookshelf?

Write one sentence to finish the story.

_____

_____

Extension: Have children create a puppet show about a contrary family that speaks only in contractions with *not*.

Macmillan/McGraw-Hill

FINDING PRONOUNS

Josie has a trumpet.
She plays it very loudly.
Tony has a violin.
He plays it very softly.
Jim and **I** have flutes.
We all play in the band.

Read the story. Underline the pronouns that you find.

1. Cheryl has a telephone.

2. She calls Keith every afternoon.

3. He calls Ruby to check on homework.

4. She calls Raoul and Philip to tell the news.

5. They call Miranda to ask about the pet geese.

6. She describes what they have done today.

7. The geese knock over Miranda's puppy, Edgar.

8. He whines and runs away.

9. She calls Cheryl with the news.

10. We will call you next.

10   Level 7/Unit 2
Pronouns

Extension: Have children repeat each sentence in the
exercise replacing the personal pronouns with the names to which
they refer.

81

Macmillan/McGraw-Hill

USING SHE, HE, IT

Remember

- A **pronoun** is a word that takes the place of one or more nouns.

- Some pronouns are **she, he, it.**

  Jill likes chocolate pudding.

  She likes **it** more than ice cream.

Look at the underlined noun. Choose the pronoun that could be used in its place. Fill in the circle next to the answer.

1. <u>Jason</u> eats nothing but spinach.

   (a.) He
   (b.) She

2. Jason loves <u>spinach</u>.

   (a.) she
   (b.) it

3. <u>Jason's mother</u> gives him lima beans.

   (a.) She
   (b.) He

4. <u>Jason</u> doesn't like lima beans.

   (a.) He
   (b.) It

5. <u>His mother</u> gives Jason canned ham.

   (a.) She
   (b.) It

6. Jason gives <u>the canned ham</u> to Roger the cat.

   (a.) he
   (b.) it

Extension: Have children continue the story of Jason, his cat, and his mother, using personal pronouns for the main characters.

Macmillan/McGraw-Hill

USING I, YOU, WE, AND THEY

Remember

- A pronoun is a word that takes the place of one or more nouns.

- Some pronouns are **I, you, we,** and **they**.

  We rode seven miles.
  You never got tired!

Circle the pronoun that completes the sentence.

1. _____ am bigger than you.
   a. I
   b. You

2. _____ are taller than me.
   a. I
   b. You

3. _____ are smaller than both of us.
   a. We
   b. They

4. _____ are the biggest kids on the block.
   a. We
   b. I

5. They live next door to _____.
   a. we
   b. you

6. _____ am riding my new bike.
   a. I
   b. You

7. _____ have new bikes, too.
   a. I
   b. They

8. _____ can all ride bikes together.
   a. We
   b. I

8 Level 7/Unit 2
Using *I, you, we,* and *they*

Extension: Have children describe life in their own neighborhoods using the pronouns in the exercise.

83

Macmillan/McGraw-Hill

USING PERSONAL PRONOUNS

Remember

• A pronoun is a word that takes the place of one or more nouns.

• Some pronouns are **she, he, it, I, you, we,** and **they**.

I am going to be a monster.
You don't scare me!

Read the sentences. Choose a pronoun from the box that could be used in each blank. Write the pronouns in the blanks.

| I | you | she | he | it | we | they |

1. Are _____ ready for Halloween?

2. _____ have my costume already.

3. What are _____ and _____ going to be for Halloween?

4. Do you think _____ is going to be a pirate?

5. First _____ are all coming to my house.

6. Then _____ will all go to the parade together.

7. Look at that pumpkin! _____ has a funny face.

8. Oh, oh! Who are _____?

Extension: Have children describe an action pantomimed by other children, using the pronouns in the exercise.

WHAT IS IT?

| Remember |

- A pronoun is a word that takes the place of one or more nouns.

- Some pronouns are **she, he, it, I, you, we**, and **they**.

It has a long pointed nose.
It has red fur.
It has a long bushy tail.
What is **it**?

Think of a person, animal, or thing.   Make up four clues about it.
Write your clues using personal pronouns.

4 Level 7/Unit 2
Writing with Pronouns

Extension: Have children read their riddles out loud, and have others
guess what they mean.

85

PRONOUNS AS SUBJECTS AND OBJECTS

I have a parrot named Feather.
My uncle gave **it** to **me**.
We have three birds altogether.
They all live with **us**.

Read the sentences. Underline the pronouns that are subjects. Circle the pronouns that are objects.

1. I take care of Feather, the parrot.

2. Feather often talks to me.

3. We cover Feather's cage at night.

4. Feather sings to us in the morning.

5. We sometimes talk back to the parrot.

6. I clean the cage and Feather flies out.

7. Feather flies away from me.

8. We once had to get Feather out of a tree.

9. The parrot looked down on us and squawked.

10. I talked to Feather while Nancy climbed the tree.

Extension: Have children write sentences that start with *I* or *we* and end with *me* or *us*.

Level 7/Unit 2

10

Macmillan/McGraw-Hill

USING I AND WE

> **Remember**
> - Use **I** and **we** in the subject part of a sentence.
> - Write **I** with a capital letter.

Read the sentences. Choose the word that belongs in the blank.
Circle your answer.

1. _____ have a great idea!
   a. I
   b. Me

2. _____ need to get some string.
   a. We
   b. Us

3. _____ will find some paper and tape.
   a. I
   b. Me

4. Can _____ find some balsa wood?
   a. we
   b. us

5. _____ will cut out the paper.
   a. I
   b. Me

6. _____ will make a frame with you.
   a. I
   b. Us

7. Then _____ will glue it all together.
   a. us
   b. we

8. You and _____ will have a new kite.
   a. I
   b. us

Macmillan/McGraw-Hill

Extension: Have children take turns making statements that start with *I* or *we*.

USING ME AND US

| Remember |

- Use **me** and **us** after an action verb.

  Did Aunt Penny see **us**?   Yes, she waved to **me**.

Read the sentences. Write the word that completes the sentence in the blank.

1. My aunt Penny is coming to
    visit _____.
    a. us
    b. we

2. She will bring _____
    some good things to eat.
    a. we
    b. us

3. She will sleep in my room
    with _____.
    a. me
    b. I

4. She will stay with _____
    for a week.
    a. us
    b. we

5. She will come to school with
    _____.
    a. I
    b. me

6. She will help _____ with
    our homework.
    a. us
    b. I

7. She will let _____ sit in
    her lap.
    a. we
    b. me

8. I love it when she visits
    _____.
    a. we
    b. me

Extension: Have children perform actions such as handing a ball to one
another, and have the receiver describe the action using *us* and *me*.

Macmillan/McGraw-Hill

NAMING YOURSELF LAST

Remember

- Name yourself last when you talk about yourself and another person.

    Morgan and I learned how to juggle.
    The clown threw the balls to **Morgan and me**.

Read the sentences. Circle the words that belong.

1. _____ are getting good at juggling.
   Morgan and I   I and Morgan

2. _____ can juggle five balls at once.
   Me and Morgan   Morgan and I

3. The circus might hire _____.
   Morgan and I   Morgan and me

4. The other jugglers have given lessons to _____.
   me and Morgan   Morgan and me

5. _____ could do a show together.
   You and I   Me and you

6. We could invite the neighbors to see _____.
   you and me   me and you

6 Level 7/Unit 2

Extension: Have children write sentences describing an afternoon
spent with a friend, naming themselves last.

89

TELLING ABOUT YOURSELF

> **Remember**
>
> - Use **I** and **we** in the subject part of a sentence.
> - Write **I** with a capital letter.
> - Use **me** and **us** after an action verb.
> - Name yourself last when you talk about yourself and another person.
>
>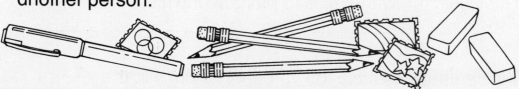

Write a letter to a pen pal from another country. Tell about yourself and your life at home and at school. Tell about your family. Tell what you do with your friends. Write at least five sentences.

_____

_____

_____

_____

_____

_____

_____

Extension: Have children send their letters to children in another country.

Level 7/Unit 2   5

VERBS AND PRONOUNS

I score a goal.

He defends the goal.

They play very well.

We win the game.

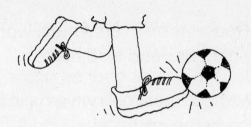

Read the sentences. Circle the verb that belongs in the sentence.

1. My sister Josie is sixteen. She **work   works** in a pizza restaurant.

2. After school she **take   takes** a bus downtown.

3. We **wait   waits** for her to get there.

4. She **serve   serves** us pizza and milk.

5. I **like   likes** pizza with peppers on it.

6. My friends are different. They **like   likes** plain cheese.

7. After we **eat   eats,** we go outside.

8. We **play   plays** until six o'clock.

Extension: Have children tell what they do after school, using pronouns for all the people they encounter.

VERBS FOR SINGULAR PRONOUNS

| Remember |

- Pronouns and verbs must work together the same way that nouns and verbs do.

- Add **s** to most action verbs in the present when you use the pronouns **he, she,** and **it.**

Grandpa **plays** tennis with me.

He **plays** very well.

It **looks** easy for him.

Read the sentences. Choose the verb that belongs in the blank. Fill in the circle next to the answer.

1. Uncle Ray is visiting. He _____ to play with me.

   (**a.**) likes

   (**b.**) like

2. He _____ lots of things for us to do together.

   (**a.**) find

   (**b.**) finds

3. Aunt Gina is here, too. She _____ my mother with the baby.

   (**a.**) help

   (**b.**) helps

4. My dad is away now. He _____ during the week.

   (**a.**) travels

   (**b.**) travel

Extension: Have children take turns making up sentences with singular pronouns for other children to finish.

Level 7/Unit 2   4

Macmillan/McGraw-Hill

VERBS FOR PLURAL PRONOUNS

Remember

- Pronouns and verbs must work together the same way that nouns and verbs do.

- Do not add **s** to most action verbs in the present when you use the pronouns **I, we, you,** and **they.**

  My aunt and uncle live in Mexico.

  They **own** a hotel.

  We **visit** them every winter.

  You **come** with us next time.

  I **want** you to come along.

Read the sentences. Choose the word that belongs in the blank. Fill in the circle next to the answer.

1. Lacy and Benny are smart. They _____ a lot.
   - **(a.)** knows
   - **(b.)** know

2. They _____ me how to use the computer.
   - **(a.)** teaches
   - **(b.)** teach

3. We _____ together after school.
   - **(a.)** study
   - **(b.)** studies

4. I _____ something every day.
   - **(a.)** learn
   - **(b.)** learns

---

4 Level 7/Unit 2

Extension: Have children work in pairs to pantomime an action while others describe what they are doing, using plural pronouns and verbs.

93

MATCHING VERBS AND PRONOUNS

Remember

- Pronouns and verbs must work together the same way that nouns and verbs do.

- Add **s** to most action verbs in the present when you use the pronouns **he, she,** and **it.**

- Do not add **s** to most action verbs in the present when you use the pronouns **I, we, you,** and **they.**

  Tiffany is happy. She **laughs** a lot.

  Phil is gloomy. He **frowns.**

  We **try** to cheer him up.

Read the sentence beginnings. Find an ending that could go with each sentence beginning. Draw a line to connect them.

1. Carmen is quick. She
2. The other team is new. They
3. Ron is tall. He
4. Cliff is a beginner. He
5. The sun is bright. It

misses the ball sometimes.

runs very fast.

find our team hard to beat.

kicks the ball over our heads.

shines in our eyes.

Extension: Have children use sentence strips to write sentences using pronouns. Have them cut them in half between pronoun and verb, mix them up, and try to reassemble them.

94

Level 7/Unit 2   5

Macmillan/McGraw-Hill

WRITING A MYSTERY STORY

| Remember |

- Pronouns and verbs must work together the same way that nouns and verbs do.

- Add **s** to most action verbs in the present when you use the pronouns **he, she,** and **it.**

- Do not add **s** to most action verbs in the present when you use the pronouns **I, we, you,** and **they.**

You are in a dark room on a gloomy night. Five people are with you. In the middle of the room is something large and mysterious. Tell a story about the people, yourself, and the mysterious thing. Use at least five of these pronouns: **I, we, he, she, it, you,** and **they.**

_____

_____

_____

_____

_____

RECOGNIZING POSSESSIVE PRONOUNS

Possessive pronouns show who or what owns something.

Is this **your** backpack?

I think it's **mine.**

It looks just like **hers**.

Read the sentences. Circle the pronouns that show possession.

1. My cousin is funny.

2. I think his jokes are great.

3. Sometimes our laughter is very loud.

4. Your sister is also funny.

5. Her stories make me laugh.

6. She tells her stories to our friends.

7. I can hear their laughter.

8. I'll tell you one of our jokes.

9. What is your opinion?

10. First, it's your turn, and then it's his turn.

Extension: Have children describe things belonging to other children using possessive pronouns.

MY, YOUR, HIS, HER

Remember

- A possessive pronoun takes the place of a possessive noun.

- It shows who or what owns something.

- Possessive pronouns include **my, your, his,** and **her.**

  Cy plays **his** clarinet.   I play **my** trumpet.
  You play **your** flute.   Myra plays **her** drums.

Read the sentences. Circle the possessive pronoun that belongs in the sentence.

1. We are riding our bikes to **your   you**   house.

2. Amy falls off **she   her** bike.

3. **She   Her** arm is not hurt.

4. Len stays on **he   his** bike.

5. I fall off **my   me** bike.

6. I think I broke **my   me** leg.

7. Amy runs to get **her   she** father.

8. I only scraped **me   my** knee.

ITS, OUR, YOUR, THEIR

Remember

- A possessive pronoun takes the place of a possessive noun.

- It shows who or what owns something.

- Possessive pronouns include **its, our, your,** and **their.**

We lost **our** kitten.   Is the kitten at **your** house?
Its ears are white.   Our neighbors lost **their** cat, too.

Read the sentences. Circle the possessive pronoun that belongs in the sentence.

1. **Our   Us**   turtles live in the same bowl.

2. My turtle pulls in   **it   its**   head.

3. **Your   You're**   turtle is wide awake.

4. It opens   **it's   its**   eyes.

5. We like to see the birds at   **your   you**   house.

6. We listen to   **they   their**   pretty chirping.

7. **You   Your**   birds are so beautiful.

8. **Our   We**   turtles are not beautiful.

98

Extension: Have children describe the belongings of others in the classroom using *your* and *their* and possessions at home using *our* and *its.*

Level 7/Unit 2   8

Macmillan/McGraw-Hill

RECOGNIZING POSSESSIVE PRONOUNS

Remember

- A possessive pronoun takes the place of a possessive noun.

- It shows who or what owns something.

- Possessive pronouns include **my, your, his, her, its, our,** and **their.**

  They moved into **their** new apartment.

  Our apartment is next door.

Read the words on the left. Then circle the words on the right that have the same meaning.

1. cat belonging to you   you cat   your cat

2. dog belonging to Pete   he dog   his dog

3. parrot belonging to the children   they parrot   their parrot

4. mouse belonging to Sheila   her mouse   she mouse

5. fish belonging to us   we fish   our fish

6. rabbit belonging to me   my rabbit   me rabbit

7. ears belonging to the rabbit   it ears   its ears

8. horse belonging to you   your horse   you're horse

---

8   Level 7/Unit 2

Extension: Have children name objects and their owners for others to supply the possessive pronoun.

USING POSSESSIVE PRONOUNS

Remember

- A possessive pronoun takes the place of a possessive noun.

- It shows who or what owns something.

- Possessive pronouns include **my, your, his, her, its, our,** and **their.**

  Here is a picture of me. Here is **my** room.

Use a word from the box to finish each sentence.

our its their his my her

1. We are going to eat _____ pizza.

2. I like pineapple, so _____ slice has pineapple on it.

3. My sister likes extra cheese, so _____ slice has more cheese.

4. My father says _____ slice is the best.

5. That slice has _____ own special sauce.

6. My mother says _____ plain slices are best.

7. This is _____ favorite place to order pizza.

8. The pizza makers make the crust in _____ own special way.

---

100 **Extension:** Have children tell about their families' favorite foods using possessive pronouns.

Level 7/Unit 2   8

RECOGNIZING ADJECTIVES

Harry is a **white** rabbit.

He has **soft** fur.

His nose is **cold** and **black**.

Read each sentence. Circle the picture that goes with the sentence.

1. Frances is a happy child.

2. Ron is a sleepy baby.

3. Nelson is an angry coach.

4. Rosi is a sad girl.

Extension: Have children use expressions for others to describe, using adjectives such as happy, sad, curious, angry, and surprised. **101**

CHOOSING ADJECTIVES

Remember

- An adjective is a word that tells about a person, place, or thing.

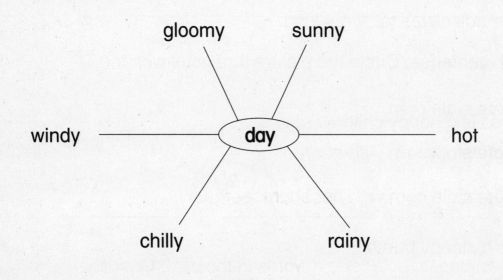

Read the sentences. Choose the adjective that belongs in the blank. Fill in the circle next to the answer.

1. I looked up at the _____ sky.
   - (a.) bright
   - (b.) rain

2. Gary started the _____ car.
   - (a.) noisy
   - (b.) rust

3. I found a _____ book.
   - (a.) pages
   - (b.) good

4. Nina climbed the _____ tree.
   - (a.) slowly
   - (b.) old

Extension: Have children hold up objects for others to describe using adjectives.

Macmillan/McGraw-Hill

WHAT KIND IS IT?

Remember

- An adjective is a word that tells about a person, place, or thing.

- Some adjectives tell what kind.

  Nelly ate corn.

  She ate **stale** corn.

  She ate **stale** corn with her teeth.

  She ate **stale** corn with her **sharp** teeth.

Read the sentences. Look at the words in the box. Choose a word to complete each sentence that tells what kind. Write the word on the line.

many	white	cozy	big

1. We had a _____ snowfall.

2. The snow was soft and _____.

3. We built a _____ igloo.

4. The snowman lasted for _____ days.

---

4   .Level 7/Unit 3

Extension: Have children hold dialogues in which one names an object, another asks what kind it is, and a third gives an adjective that answers the question.

HOW MANY ARE THERE?

Remember

- An adjective is a word that tells about a person, place, or thing.

- Some adjectives tell how many.

  Terry ate **ten** pancakes.

  She drank **three** glasses of milk.

Read each sentence. Choose the word from the box that tells how many there are. Write the number on the line.

| one two three four five six seven |

1. Polly saw _____ geese.

2. Ken wants _____ dollars.

3. Tad caught _____ fish.

4. Pat scored _____ goals.

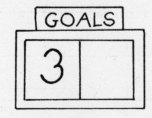

Extension: Have children hold up a number of objects (between one and ten), and ask others to make up sentences telling how many there are.

104

Level 7/Unit 3

4

Macmillan/McGraw-Hill

DESCRIBING WHAT YOU SEE

| Remember |

- An adjective is a word that tells about a person, place, or thing.

- Some adjectives tell what kind.

- Some adjectives tell how many.

  Ira has a **tiny** eraser.

  Lisa has **two** pencils.

Look at the people in the picture. Look at the things they have. Name the things and describe them with an adjective.

Ada   Lisa   Randy

Example Lisa has a **long** hot dog.

1. Lisa has a _____ vest.

2. Randy has a _____ cap.

3. Ada has a _____ bag of peanuts.

4. Ada has _____ hair.

RECOGNIZING ARTICLES

Words like **a, an,** and **the** are called articles.

Pamela has **a** softball.

She hits **the** ball to center field.

It is **an** out.

Read each sentence. Circle the articles **a, an,** and **the.**

1. Ricky is a giant frog.

2. He lives in the forest.

3. The forest is cool and damp.

4. Ricky is a slippery animal.

5. He has a long tongue.

6. He eats an insect.

7. He sits on a rock.

8. He leaps over the leaves.

9. He crawls under a log.

10. An ape smiles at Ricky.

Extension: Have children make a list of items in the classroom, using
a, an, or **the** before each noun.

Level 7/Unit 3   10

USING *THE* BEFORE A NOUN

Remember

- The words **a, an,** and **the** are special adjectives.

- Use **the** before a noun that names one or more than one.

  the pencil   **the** window

  the clocks   **the** desks

Read each pair of sentences.
Circle the sentence that is correct.

1. Wilson saw the elephants.

   Wilson saw a elephants.

2. Lateesha read newspaper.

   Lateesha read the newspaper.

3. Chloe found the missing gloves.

   Chloe found a missing gloves.

4. Jake ate bagel.

   Jake ate the bagel.

5. Ali chose movie.

   Ali chose the movie.

Extension: Have children describe well-known places near the school, such as the store or the bus stop using the word the.

USING *AN* BEFORE A NOUN

Remember

- The words **a, an,** and **the** are special adjectives.

- Use **a** or **an** before a noun that names one person, place, or thing.

- Use **an** before a word that begins with a vowel sound.

    an egg   **an** apple

Read the sentences. Look at the words in the box. Choose a word to complete each sentence. Write the word on the line.

banana	usher	man	apple	monkey	sea
ox	drawer	ape	oven	ocean	cow

1. Karen sees an _____ at the zoo.

2. Steve puts the bread into an _____.

3. The ship sails over an _____.

4. An _____ shows me to a seat.

5. The plow is pulled by an _____.

6. It is good to eat an _____ every day.

Extension: Have children make up new sentences using the words they wrote.

Macmillan/McGraw-Hill

USING A BEFORE A NOUN

Remember

- The words **a, an,** and **the** are special adjectives.

- Use **a** or **an** before a noun that names one person, place, or thing.

- Use **a** before a word that begins with a consonant sound.

  a chicken   **a** train   **a** barn

Read the sentences. Choose the article that belongs in the blank. Fill in the circle next to the answer.

1. Pia has _____ telephone.

   a.) an

   b.) a

2. She plans to call _____ friend.

   a.) an

   b.) a

3. She wants to go for _____ hike.

   a.) an

   b.) a

4. Pia calls Tom and sets up _____ time to meet.

   a.) a

   b.) an

5. Pia and Tom climb up _____ mountain.

   a.) an

   b.) a

6. When they get to the top, they take _____ rest.

   a.) an

   b.) a

---

6 Level 7/Unit 3

Extension: Have children name the objects in or on their desks, using *a* before each one that starts with a consonant sound.

Macmillan/McGraw-Hill

USING A, AN, AND *THE* IN SENTENCES

> **Remember**
>
> • The words **a, an,** and **the** are special adjectives.
>
> • Use **a** or **an** before a noun that names one person, place, or thing.
>
> • Use **a** before a word that begins with a consonant sound.
>
> • Use **an** before a word that begins with a vowel sound.
>
> • Use **the** before a noun that names one or more than one.
>
> **The** letters are in **an** envelope on **a** table.

Write six sentences. Use one of the words with the correct special adjective that goes with the word in each sentence.

earth	sun	boy	girl	children	apple

_____

_____

_____

_____

_____

Extension: Have children use the following words in sentences: *antelope, alligators,* and *tiger.*

Level 7/Unit 3

6

RECOGNIZING ADJECTIVES THAT COMPARE

Toya is tall.

Donna is tall**er** than Toya.

Read each sentence. Underline the adjectives that compare.

1. Troy is shorter than Ken.

2. Ann is taller than Rob.

3. A rock is harder than a rubber ball.

4. Kim is quicker than Chet.

5. Chet runs faster than I do.

6. A cat is softer than a cow.

7. Donna is older than Trudy.

8. Trudy is younger than Joy.

9. It is colder today than yesterday.

10. Pat is stronger than John.

Extension: Have children compare two objects in their possession,
saying which is longer, older, heavier, and so on.

USING *ER* IN COMPARISONS

Remember

- Add **er** to compare two people, places, or things.

    My story is long.   My story is long**er**!

Read the sentences. Look at the words in the box. Choose a word to complete each sentence. Write the word on the line.

smaller	taller	quieter	kinder
quicker	older	smarter	softer

1. My cat is _____ than Kara's cat.

2. Kara's cat is _____ than Gabe's dog.

3. Gabe's dog is _____ than Todd's dog.

4. Todd's dog is _____ than Caty's pig.

5. Caty's pig is _____ than Vera's horse.

6. Vera's horse is _____ than Maggie's pony.

7. Maggie's pony is _____ than Jeff's goat.

8. Jeff's goat is _____ than Fran's turtle.

Extension: Have children compare pictures of people, animals, objects, or places using comparative adjectives.

Macmillan/McGraw-Hill

USING *EST* IN COMPARISONS

Remember

- Add **est** to an adjective to compare more than two people, places, or things.

  Tim's horn is loud.   Mike's horn is louder.

  Ray's horn is loud**est**.

Look at the pictures. Then read the sentences. Think of a comparative word that could be used in each blank. Write the word in the blank.

1.    Rene is the _____ girl.

2.    Jim is the _____ runner.

3.    The dog is the _____ animal.

4.    Mom is the _____.

Extension: Have children draw three similar people or animals and then make comparisons among them, using words that end in *est*.   **113**

USING *ER* AND *EST* IN COMPARISONS

| Remember |

- You can use adjectives to compare people, places, or things.

- Add **er** to compare two people, places, or things.

- Add **est** to compare more than two people, places, or things.

cold colder coldest

Read the questions. Circle the picture that answers each question.

1. Which one is the smallest?

2. Which one is the tallest?

3. Who is older?

4. Which one is shorter?

Extension: Have children draw pictures and ask questions of each other similar to those in the exercise.

Level 7/Unit 3   4

Macmillan/McGraw-Hill

WRITING A FAIRY TALE

Remember

- Add **er** to an adjective to compare two people, places, or things.

- Add **est** to an adjective to compare more than two people, places, or things.

rich	rich**er**	rich**est**

bright	bright**er**	bright**est**

Write a story about three dragons—one long, one longer, and the last one the longest. Tell about their adventures. Use at least five words that end with **er** and **est**.

Once upon a time...._____

_____

_____

_____

_____

_____

Extension: Have children illustrate their stories and collect them in a classroom book.

RECOGNIZING ADVERBS

An adverb tells about a verb.

The firefighters run **quickly**.

The doctor called **yesterday**.

We play **near** the grass.

Read the sentences. Underline the word that tells more about each verb.

1. The sun will soon rise.

2. Ginny wakes up early.

3. Then she sits up quickly.

4. She barely hears a sound.

5. Quickly she looks at her cat.

6. The cat sleeps soundly.

7. Quietly she opens the tent flap.

8. Suddenly she sees a beautiful doe.

Extension: Have children pantomime actions, and have others tell what they are doing, using adverbs to describe the actions more thoroughly.

Level 7/Unit 3

8

Macmillan/McGraw-Hill

WHEN?

| Remember |

- An adverb tells more about a verb.

- Some adverbs tell when.
  Is it raining **now**?   No. It will rain **later.**

Write a word from the box to complete each sentence.

| today   yesterday   later   Soon   now   Once |

1. After we went to the park _____, we came
   home to rest.

2. Then we watched a movie_____ in the
   evening.

3. Yesterday, it was cloudy, but _____ it will
   be sunny.

4. Right _____, the sky is clear.

5. _____ we will go outside.

6. _____ it gets dark, we will have to go
   inside.

Extension: Have children ask each other questions about when
something happened and answer using adverbs of time.

WHERE?

Remember

- An adverb tells more about a verb.

- Some adverbs tell when.

- Some adverbs tell where.

   Did Paul go **out**?   No. He stayed **in**.

Use a word from the box below to finish each sentence.

out	up	in	forward	down	near

1. The bird flew from the ground _____ into the tree.

2. Did that sound come from _____ or far?

3. The sign fell _____ in the strong wind.

4. The dog walked _____ the door into the yard.

5. The car moved _____ when we pushed it.

6. It is raining! Please come _____ the house.

Extension: Have children pantomime answers to questions that ask
where: in, out, up, down, and so on.

Macmillan/McGraw-Hill

How?

> Remember
> • An adverb tells more about a verb.
> • Some adverbs tell how.
>
> Felina reads very **quickly**.

Read the sentences. Look at the underlined word. Write the word as an adverb that tells how.

1. George thinks very <u>quick</u>.   _____

2. He jumps up <u>sudden</u>.   _____

3. He grabs Tom's arm <u>firm</u>.   _____

4. Tom yells <u>loud</u>.   _____

5. George smiles <u>broad</u>.   _____

6. He looks around <u>wild</u>.   _____

7. He turns around <u>slow</u>.   _____

8. Tom stands <u>quiet</u>.   _____

9. George laughs <u>odd</u>.   _____

10. Then he disappears <u>mysterious</u>.   _____

---

10   Level 7/Unit 3
     Adverbs Telling How

Extension: Have children describe a television or movie scene they
remember, using adverbs to tell about how the action took place.

119

Macmillan/McGraw-Hill

WRITING ABOUT AN EVENT

> ### Remember
>
> • An adverb tells more about a verb.
> • An adverb can tell when, where, or how.
>
> Jason raced **there quickly.**
> He is returning **now.**

Laurel has written a news story. Help Laurel make it more exciting by putting in adverbs that tell when, where, and how.

_____ some zoo animals escaped!
   when
People rushed _____ to see what was happening.
          how
Zebras ran _____ outside their fence.
     how
The zookeepers chased them _____.
            where
_____ the zookeepers blew their whistles _____.
  when   how
The animals stopped. The people stood _____.
          how
_____ the zookeepers led the animals back _____.
  when   where
The people cheered _____. The animals were safe.
        how

---

120 **Extension:** Have children exchange papers and compare the adverbs they chose.

Level 7/Unit 3
Writing About an Event

10